This book belongs to ...

_____

THE ACTION BIBLE

Christmas

25 Stories about Jesus' Arrival

DAVID C COOK

transforming lives together

THE ACTION BIBLE CHRISTMAS
Published by David C Cook
4050 Lee Vance Drive
Colorado Springs, CO 80918 U.S.A.

Integrity Music Limited, a Division of David C Cook
Brighton, East Sussex BN1 2RE, England

The graphic circle C logo is a registered trademark of David C Cook.

Library of Congress Control Number 2022930350
ISBN 978-0-8307-8464-6
eISBN 978-0-8307-8465-3

The Team: Amy Konyndyk, Stephanie Bennett, Judy Gillispie, Parker Bennett,
Jeff Gerke, Vicki Kuyper, James Hershberger, Susan Murdock
Cover Design: James Hershberger

Printed in Canada
First Edition 2022

1 2 3 4 5 6 7 8 9 10

041422

Contents

The Christmas Story

Luke 1:26–38; 2:1–20

In the sixth month of Elizabeth's pregnancy, God sent the angel Gabriel to Nazareth, a town in Galilee, to a virgin pledged to be married to a man named Joseph, a descendant of David. The virgin's name was Mary. The angel went to her and said, "Greetings, you who are highly favored! The Lord is with you."

Mary was greatly troubled at his words and wondered what kind of greeting this might be. But the angel said to her, "Do not be afraid, Mary; you have found favor with God. You will conceive and give birth to a son, and you are to call him Jesus. He will be great and will be called the Son of the Most High. The Lord God will give him the throne of his father David, and he will reign over Jacob's descendants forever; his kingdom will never end."

"How will this be," Mary asked the angel, "since I am a virgin?"

The angel answered, "The Holy Spirit will come on you, and the power of the Most High will overshadow you. So the holy one to be born will be called the Son of God. Even Elizabeth your relative is going to have a child in her old age, and she who was said to be unable to conceive is in her sixth month. For no word from God will ever fail."

"I am the Lord's servant," Mary answered. "May your word to me be fulfilled." Then the angel left her.

In those days Caesar Augustus issued a decree that a census should be taken of the entire Roman world. (This was the first census that took place while Quirinius was governor of Syria.) And everyone went to their own town to register.

So Joseph also went up from the town of Nazareth in Galilee to Judea, to Bethlehem the town of David, because he belonged to the house and line of David. He went there to register with Mary, who was pledged to be married to him and was expecting a child. While they were there, the time came for the baby to be born, and she gave birth to her firstborn, a son. She wrapped him in cloths and placed him in a manger, because there was no guest room available for them.

And there were shepherds living out in the fields nearby, keeping watch over their flocks at night. An angel of the Lord appeared to them, and the glory of the Lord shone around them, and they were terrified. But the angel said to them, "Do not be afraid. I bring you good news that will cause great joy for all the people. Today in the town of David a Savior has been born to you; he is the Messiah, the Lord. This will be a sign to you: You will find a baby wrapped in cloths and lying in a manger."

Suddenly a great company of the heavenly host appeared with the angel, praising God and saying,

"Glory to God in the highest heaven,
    and on earth peace to those on whom his favor rests."

When the angels had left them and gone into heaven, the shepherds said to one another, "Let's go to Bethlehem and see this thing that has happened, which the Lord has told us about."

So they hurried off and found Mary and Joseph, and the baby, who was lying in the manger. When they had seen him, they spread the word concerning what had been told them about this child, and all who heard it were amazed at what the shepherds said to them. But Mary treasured up all these things and pondered them in her heart. The shepherds returned, glorifying and praising God for all the things they had heard and seen, which were just as they had been told.

1

Isaiah

Almighty God, I want to understand.

You have shown me things that have yet to happen. I don't know when they will occur, but I trust that they will someday. You've given me glimpses of Your plans for Your people—and for a special person You're sending: the Messiah. I admit, when I line up all Your promises about Him, they don't really make sense. How could one person be and do so many things?

For example, why would You have this Messiah born in little old Bethlehem? Shouldn't a king come from a mighty city? But I suppose our greatest king, David, was from Bethlehem, and You said the Messiah will be from David's family line. You also said this chosen One will bring Your light from Galilee—and that's so far from Bethlehem. I don't see how that fits together.

You give this man royal titles—Your very own titles! Mighty God and Everlasting Father and Prince of Peace. That shows He must indeed come straight from You. But then it sounds like He will be a servant, instead of a king who deserves others to serve Him. You said He will open the eyes of the blind and heal the sick and bring joyful freedom to people in chains. He sounds compassionate and humble.

So why will He be punished? These sad visions You've given me … I see His suffering and pain, and I just don't understand. How could Your special servant be rejected, beaten, and killed? Won't Your people grasp that You Yourself have sent Him?

The vision I've seen shows that He will be a perfect sacrifice—to take on our wrongdoing so our sins can be forgiven. His punishment will bring us peace, and His wounds will heal our souls.

I'm so glad Your vision doesn't end there … because You don't let the Messiah remain in death. After He is buried in a rich man's tomb, You will bring Him to life again—forever. And the good news of Your salvation will reach to the ends of the earth!

Almighty God, Your ways are high above mine. You know I will continue to tell Your people what You have planned … even when I myself can't put it all together. I know some day it will all make sense … and You will fulfill Your promises, even if it takes centuries.

What do you think it was like for Isaiah to hear from God?

If you met a prophet like Isaiah, what would you ask him?

What are your favorite prophecies about the Messiah that Isaiah mentioned?

2
Zechariah

Why didn't I believe the angel?

For all the years of our marriage, my precious wife, Elizabeth, and I have prayed for a son. I have served faithfully in the temple, and she is a good wife who loves the Lord. But still, we have no children. During all that time, I have kept serving at the temple in Jerusalem, trying not to question the plans of the Lord.

Then, when I am an old man and Elizabeth is beyond the age of childbearing, I finally get chosen for the greatest honor of a priest. I tended the altar of incense, mere inches from the Most Holy Place.

And an angel appeared—the most majestic thing I'd ever seen—as if he'd been there forever. And he told me not to be afraid. Ah yes—don't be afraid. Of course, it was *terrifying*! He said my prayer for a son had been heard. God heard *me*?

The angel said we would have a son. But who am I? Am I like Abraham from generations long ago, that God would give me a son in my old age? And who is Elizabeth—like his wife, Sarah?

I realize now I should've jumped for joy! I should've hugged the angel—well, probably not. But I certainly should've thanked God for blessing us with a son, and for announcing him in the temple!

But what *did* I do? I questioned. I doubted that God could bring life from two people as old as us. I questioned the angel Gabriel, who stood in front of me after standing before God Himself.

So … the angel silenced me, and I've not been able to speak since that day—months ago. I mistakenly thought God was unable to hear me all those years, and now people truly *are* unable to hear me. Ah, the Lord has a sense of humor. I am thankful He simply shut my mouth instead of striking me with lightning for my lack of faith.

Now my sweet Elizabeth *is* pregnant! She's carrying our child, a son we will name John, as the angel commanded.

If I ever speak again, my first words—and all my words from that day forward—will be words of praise for the God who hears the prayers of His people.

Why might Zechariah have been afraid of the angel?

What would be the benefit of John having older parents?

What do you think Elizabeth thought when Zechariah couldn't speak?

3
Gabriel

"Don't be afraid!" I know that's an odd way to begin a conversation, but I've found it's something I usually need to say with every message God has me deliver. I guess seeing an angel for the very first time can be a little frightening for a human being. But I'm just delivering information from God, kind of like a heavenly postman—with wings! The funny thing is that right now *I'm* the one who's feeling a little nervous. I think I'm just excited because the news God asked me to deliver announces the most wonderful thing that has happened since God created the world!

But where are my manners? First, let me introduce myself. Angels have names, just like people. Mine is Gabriel, which means "God is my strength." But today God has asked me to deliver the tenderest of news—a birth announcement. This isn't the first time I've visited someone to tell her she's going to have a baby. Just a few months ago, I told Zechariah that he and his wife, Elizabeth, would soon be parents. Today I get to tell Elizabeth's relative, a teenage girl named Mary, that she will give birth to a Son as well!

But unlike my message for Zechariah, who is very old and had prayed for years to become a father, this message may not be welcome news. After all, Mary is engaged but not yet married, so this will certainly be a surprise. And even though Mary will be the baby's mother, the baby's father won't be Joseph, the man she's engaged to marry. The baby's father will be God Himself! I know this all sounds a little confusing, and that's totally understandable. Nothing like this has ever happened before!

I should know. I've been around a long time—as far as people count things. More than six hundred years ago, I helped a man named Daniel understand a dream God gave him. More than seven hundred years ago, God spoke to the prophet Isaiah in a vision. I might not have been God's chosen messenger on that day, but every angel in heaven knows about God's promise to send His people a Savior. Now the time has come for God to deliver on His promise. I hope I can help Mary understand her important role in God's amazing plan. I wonder what she's going to say?

Would you like to see an angel? Why or why not?

Why do you think God used angels like Gabriel to deliver messages to people?

If God sent an angel to give you a message, what do you think it might be?

4
Mary

My life has always been a quiet one. I grew up in Nazareth in the same house where I was born, with the same friends, the same familiar view of the surrounding hills, and a picture in my head of what my future would look like when I had a family of my own. But ever since an angel of God visited me, my simple life has been turned upside down!

I still don't understand it all, but one thing I know for sure: I am blessed! God has chosen me, just an ordinary girl, to be part of His extraordinary plan. The angel Gabriel's news fills me with so much joy that I simply have to sing!

> My soul gives glory to the Lord.
>   My spirit delights in God my Savior.
> He has taken note of me
>   even though I am not considered important.
> From now on all people will call me blessed.
>   The Mighty One has done great things for me.
>   His name is holy. (Luke 1:46–49 NIRV)

I think I'll be singing songs of thanks and praise to God right up to the moment this child is born—and every day after that! I know I'm young, but I'm so excited to be a mother … to hold my Son in my arms, to hear Him speak His first words and see Him take His first steps, to play hide-and-seek with Him in the olive groves! I haven't met Him yet, but I already love Him. I don't know how being a mother to God's Son will be different from raising any other child, but I'm excited to find out.

I know that even though what lies ahead will be wonderful, it'll be difficult too. Joseph will be a good father to our child. God has provided well for my family. But I'm holding especially tight to the last words Gabriel said to me: "Nothing is impossible with God." I've always known in my heart that was true, but now what seems impossible is actually happening to *me*! My life may have been turned upside down, but it's God's way of turning the world right side up again, of drawing people back to Himself. Yes, I am blessed. I just hope that when I tell Joseph, he feels the same way …

When have you felt so happy you wanted to sing? What made you feel that way?

What is something that's hard for you but you know you can do with God's help?

What do you think it would be like if your parents raised God's Son in your home?

5
Joseph

I'm going to tell you something you may not believe. I'm still getting used to the idea myself! My new wife, Mary, is going to give birth to God's Son, and I get to help raise Him here on earth!

Why was I chosen? I'm just a simple carpenter living in Nazareth. It wasn't long ago that I was engaged to Mary and our families were preparing for our wedding. We were looking forward to living as husband and wife, but that was still a little ways off. Honestly, I was still getting used to that idea too.

Then one day Mary nervously told me that she was pregnant. Since we weren't together yet as husband and wife, I knew the child wasn't mine. Mary carefully explained how an angel had visited her. He told her the baby was actually God's Son from the Holy Spirit. At first nothing made sense. I mean, did angels still visit people like that? I thought only prophets could see angels. I could tell she was watching me closely to see if I would believe her, but she was so peaceful about everything.

That night, I was lying in bed, trying to decide what to do. I didn't want Mary to be shamed or punished, so I thought maybe I could just quietly call off our wedding. Then I had the most vivid dream! This time an angel appeared to *me* and told me Mary's child really *was* the Son of God! The angel instructed me to take Mary as my wife and to name the baby Jesus. He also said that one day this Son would save all God's people from their sins!

So what did I do? Why, I did exactly what the angel said! I went to Mary and told her what I'd heard. I apologized for not believing her, but Mary said she was so happy I still wanted to be her husband. She seemed so confident that God was providing for everything. Not long after that, we had our wedding. Now I'm taking care of Mary, and we're waiting for God's Son to be born. What an honor! I don't know what God has in store for the three of us, but I know that He will protect us— and also that one day His Son is going to do incredible things!

What do you think Joseph was like as a dad?

How do you think Joseph felt when he met an angel in a dream?

How would you feel being an earthly relative to Jesus?

6

Elizabeth

I see a woman *way* in the distance.

My eyes are not so good anymore, as I am very old, and I am expecting no visitors today, so I sit on a stool in the shade to wait for her. I fold a swaddling blanket in my lap, and I slowly rub my belly, happily thinking of the baby I'm carrying.

What joy I have that I will soon be a mother!

It's wrong for people to think that if a woman can't have a baby, it's because she has sinned—or because God is mad at her! Do they forget Sarah, Rebekah, and Rachel in the Scriptures? They too were childless for years, but not for any sin of theirs. God was waiting for His own timing.

An angel appeared before *my husband*, Zechariah, and told him that I would have a baby. A son who would be great in the eyes of the Most High! I believe it. Each day I try to wait patiently for this child to arrive. I know God's promise to us will be true, for He is faithful. So I wait … What are a few more months after so many years?

The woman is closer now; she is young. "Shalom," she calls and waves. It is my dear relative, Mary, come all the way from Nazareth. What a lovely surprise!

"Mary? Is it you?"

She hurries to me. "Auntie Elizabeth!"

I rise to meet her, but when she says my name, I feel my son inside me move! I put my hand to my belly in surprise.

"What is it, Auntie?" Mary cries, carefully guiding me back down to my stool.

A flash of knowledge possible only from God comes upon me. It's as if I can see the angel Gabriel appearing not only to Zechariah in the temple but also to sweet Mary in her home. Suddenly I understand that I am not the only woman carrying a miraculous baby.

"Mary! God has blessed you more than other women. And blessed is the child you will have! But why is God so kind to me? Why has the mother of my Lord come to me?" (Luke 1:42–43 NIRV).

She looks amazed that I could know her secret. I can't wait to tell her my story and hear all about hers.

Who is your favorite relative to visit?

Why do you think Mary went to stay with Elizabeth?

What's something you've always wanted but may never receive?

7

Joseph's Friend

I'm still a little confused by everything that has happened—with Joseph, I mean.

Joseph and I have known each other as long as I can remember. When we were kids, we used to sit together and listen to the rabbi teach us from God's Word. We became men around the same time, and Joseph got engaged to Mary just a few weeks after my wife and me. As we grew up, we each inherited the same jobs as our fathers. Joseph learned to be a carpenter, and I practiced to become a rope maker. Joseph and I were still friends, but we were so busy we didn't see each other as much as we used to.

Then one day Joseph said we really needed to talk. He seemed both excited and a little overwhelmed. I asked him if everything was okay. He finally told me that Mary, his fiancée, is pregnant but he isn't the baby's father. Naturally, I was shocked. How could that be? But it gets even stranger. Joseph said that the baby is the child of God and that he and Mary are going to parent God's Son together. I was so startled, I almost choked!

Joseph and Mary have always been sweethearts, but all this seems really weird. I have so many questions … Is Mary *really* going to be the mother of God's Son? What's so special about *her*? And why Joseph? He's a great guy and all, but raising the child of God? Is he up to the task? After all, being a parent is hard enough. Imagine your child is the Son of God! So much pressure to raise Him right!

I'm just glad *my* wife hasn't told me anything like that. Both of us are just looking forward to raising our children here in Nazareth, like we were raised. Nazareth is a nice town, and I'm glad not much happens around here.

Then again, I heard people saying the Romans might be taking a new census soon. I wonder what that's all about …

Would you want to have the same job as your mom or dad when you grow up?

Imagine you were Joseph's friend. What would you say to him after everything he told you?

How do you feel about maybe being a mom or dad someday?

8
Census Announcer

"Make way for the messenger of the Roman Empire!" I feel so powerful whenever I say that.

As a Roman messenger, I have a very important job: I am responsible for carrying Caesar's decrees all across his mighty empire. Long ago these lands were just tiny little countries with no leader, but now they're united under the rule of Caesar Augustus! They ought to be thankful!

I've been all around the Roman world, and I've seen many different regions. As the empire grows larger and more powerful, I have more places to visit and more people to take messages to. My arrival reminds people of Caesar's mighty authority, since not everyone likes Rome as much as I do.

Some of these people still cling to their old customs and beliefs. Take the Jews, for instance. They still believe a Messiah will come and defeat their enemies. Ha! Surely they don't consider *us* their enemies. I highly doubt their God could overthrow us. We are Romans after all!

Speaking of the Jews, I'm traveling throughout Galilee, on my way to a nowhere town called Nazareth to deliver an important decree: Caesar has just announced a new census! Caesar wants all his subjects to be counted so he knows exactly how many people he is in charge of and how much he can expect from taxes. What a splendid idea! And to make it easier for us to count everyone, each man must return to the town where his ancestors are from. For some people, that may be very far away. Still, if Caesar says they must go, they will go. That is our law.

Phew! I sure am hot with the sun and the layers of official gear I have to wear. I'm just glad I have a horse to carry me from place to place. Imagine how terrible it would be to have to *walk* all this way! It would refresh me to take off some of this heavy uniform, but if I did that, I would look weak. Rome must never be allowed to look weak, so neither can I. Still, it's hard to always look strong and important.

Soon I will arrive in Nazareth and make my announcement to the people there: "Make way for the messenger of the Roman Empire!"

How do you think God's people felt about the Roman Empire?

How do you feel when you're pushed around by people more powerful than you?

The Romans thought Caesar was more powerful than God. What do you say and why?

9
Mary's Friend

My best friend just told me some very special news! Of course, Mary and I have shared everything with each other over the years, ever since we were little girls playing and hiding in the olive groves and learning to cook from our mommas. But this news is different. This news—it's a little harder to believe.

I already knew Mary was going to have a baby. She told me. We spend a lot of time together, and I could tell something was on her mind. But the other day she finally told me that God Himself, not her husband-to-be, Joseph, is the baby's father—and that an angel visited her and told her the good news. How could that be? But I know Mary would never make up stories. She's always been the kindest, most truthful person I've ever met.

We've grown up together, side by side, as close as sisters. She was the one with the thick, dark curls twisting like a grapevine around her shoulders. I was the one with the light-brown braid falling straight down my back like a barley stalk. Other than our hair, we were so alike in every way that we almost seemed to share the same soul.

For years we've whispered and giggled together, planning what our futures would be like. We shared our dreams about who we'd marry, how many children we'd have, and how we'd always live right next door to each other so that our daughters could grow up to be best friends, just like us. I thought that dream was going to come true when Mary got engaged to Joseph. But maybe God has given her a different dream.

Today Mary's leaving for Bethlehem, with Joseph, to be counted for the census. This will be the farthest she's ever been from home without her family—and without me. And she's so close to her delivery time. I can tell she's scared. I want to be excited for her, but I don't think our futures will look anything like we thought. I also have an uneasy feeling that this is just the beginning of her journey, that God has plans that will lead her even further from all that is familiar. But I love Mary and want God's best for her. I know I can trust God to be an even better friend to Mary than she's been to me.

What makes your friend so special to you?

If you were Mary's friend, what are ways you might respond and rejoice with her?

How has God been a friend to you?

10
Traveler

Those greedy Romans! They just won't give us a break!

As if taking over and forcing us to pay taxes wasn't bad enough, now Caesar is sending everyone back to his ancestor's hometown for a census of his entire empire. If only I hadn't been born so far away. I've already been walking for days, and I'm not even halfway there!

Why couldn't the Romans just count us where we live right now? Don't they care about us at all? Ah, who am I kidding? The Romans just want to tax us and keep us under their authority. This whole census is probably just to remind us that they're the ones in charge. What a bunch of bullies!

It's dangerous to make this kind of journey alone, so I'm thankful there are plenty of other travelers on the road to keep me company. Most of us are just anxious to get where we're going, be counted, and then get back home—to our jobs and families.

I spoke to a kind young man on the road yesterday. We met as we rested at a well. He and his wife were heading to Bethlehem from Nazareth. Talk about a long journey! And what's more, his young wife was pregnant! Imagine that—you're getting ready to have a baby but you have to pack up and travel all the way to another town.

I feel pretty sorry for both of them. The woman was riding a donkey, and her husband was walking alongside her. It can be so tiring and stressful out on the road, and she looked thirsty, but she kept asking her husband if *he* needed to stop and rest for a while. What a sweet thing to say!

I eventually moved on, as I was heading in the opposite direction. Since I'm alone, I can travel faster. I hope they make it to Bethlehem all right. I see that a lot of people are heading toward Jerusalem for the census, and the towns and villages nearby are going to be packed. It seems that man and his wife aren't going to arrive as soon as the others. I just hope they can find somewhere to rest tonight. Please, God, help them find a place to stay …

Can you imagine life without cars? What would it be like?

How would you feel if you saw Mary and Joseph on the road to Bethlehem? What would you say to them?

When have you prayed for God to help someone else?

11

Town of Bethlehem

Welcome to Bethlehem! That's me—a really old town just a handful of miles south of Jerusalem.

I've been around many generations. Some call me "the city of David" because King David was born here. And David lived more than a thousand years ago! Since then, more and more people have moved here. People enjoy coming to visit me, and I'm mentioned numerous times in the Scriptures.

When you come, the first thing you'll see is a lot of big, sloping hills. I'm actually located at the top of a hill myself. Once you get past all those hills, you'll see some of the buildings where people work and live. Most shelters around here are built out of stone. We don't get much rain, so the roofs are all flat. People can walk around on top of the buildings and watch travelers as they approach the town.

Most of my people are very friendly, and they're happy to have visitors—except for the Romans. Whenever a Roman soldier comes to visit, the people get really quiet and nervous. Everyone is afraid the Romans will punish them if they don't act respectfully and say nice things about Caesar.

I remember before the Romans arrived. Things were a lot more peaceful back then. Now everyone is coming and going, thanks to a census, or count of the people, that the Romans are taking. I've seen some people leave my walls, and I've seen even more people come rushing in, looking for a place to stay. There have been a lot of feet walking along my narrow dirt streets. I'm glad to have new people come to visit me; I just wish they were happier to be here.

It's dark now that the sun has set, and all the homes are lit from inside with oil lamps. Soon everyone will be asleep—everyone except two weary travelers and their donkey. They arrived about an hour ago, and they've been walking all around, from building to building, looking for a place to stay. I must have some room somewhere! Maybe an inn or a house or …

Bethlehem is a very old town. What is the oldest place you've ever visited?

Imagine if your town could talk. What kinds of things do you think it would say?

What place from the Bible would you most like to visit? Why?

12

Innkeeper

As if things around here couldn't get any crazier, now I've got a couple of travelers out in the stable, and they're about to have a baby!

This all started because of that census the rotten Romans are taking. People have been walking all across Israel, trying to get back to wherever they're from. It's been a big mess!

I guess Bethlehem is the ancestral home to more people than I thought. There's a whole crowd of travelers who are staying here in town while the Romans do their counting. I mean, we even have people coming from *Nazareth*! That crazy place? But hey, it's good for business. After all, these travelers all need a place to stay, and since I run an inn, I've been setting people up with rooms all week long. By the time the sun went down today, all my rooms were full again.

Then suddenly, just as I was getting ready to go to bed, this young couple came to my door. The husband told me his wife was about to give birth to her first child, and he practically begged for a place to stay for the night. Naturally, I wanted to help, but what could I do? I didn't have any rooms to spare, and I couldn't just throw someone else out on the street.

Then I got this feeling … I'm not sure where it came from, but I thought I heard a little voice inside my head. It was telling me one thing: *stable.*

That's it! I thought. *They can stay in the stable for the night!* Sure, it'll be a little crowded with all the animals (and maybe a bit smelly too), but if this woman is going to have a baby, she's got to have some kind of roof over her head.

My wife was very busy with our paying guests, but she suggested a couple of things they might need as I helped the couple settle their things in the stable. By then the woman was getting really close to having her baby. That was only a few minutes ago. I sure hope everything is all right out there. Those people seem nice and very tired. I hope their baby arrives safely.

What would be a benefit to sleeping in a stable with animals?

Have you ever relied on the kindness of a stranger in an emergency? How did that feel?

Why do you think God sent His Son to be born in these surroundings?

13
Manger

I wasn't designed to be a cradle. Since the world was created, I was just another hunk of limestone lying in a field. But one day, someone who lives nearby noticed me. Well, he noticed several things about me: I was too big to conveniently move, I was lying right where he wanted to build a shelter for his animals, and I was a useful shape. So what did he do? He fashioned me into a feeding trough, a manger.

In some parts of the world, mangers are made of wood. But this region has more rocks than trees. So he left me right where I'd always been and built the stable around me. Then, ever so patiently, he chipped away at my hard surface to make a bowl-shaped hollow. Since then, I've been serving up dinner for the donkeys, cows, and sheep inside this drafty old stable. It's not a great job, but if you're a rock, holding feed for messy, slobbering, stinky animals is more interesting than just standing around in the same place day after day, eroding in the wind and rain.

But today I am a cradle! I hold a newborn baby! His skin is so soft and warm, I feel rather embarrassed about the dirty, cold surface of my hard stone. Now I'm thankful that the constant munching of animals' muzzles has worn the bottom of my trough almost smooth over time.

I've seen plenty of animals give birth through the years. But I'd never witnessed a human baby take its first breath inside these walls, let alone one they're calling the Son of God! To hold something so precious, well … it's a day I'll never forget! Today I'm more than just a rock. Today I'm holy ground!

Of course, I'd like to think God holds a special place in His heart for rocks. After all, He carved His laws, the Ten Commandments, on us! Rocks have served as altars and temple walls. God used one small stone thrown by David to bring down Goliath. And now, look at me! I'm a bed for God's Son! I may not have been designed to be a cradle, but I was destined to be one. As the mother who gave birth tonight kept saying, over and over again, "Nothing is impossible with God."

Would you rather sleep in your bed or in a stone feeding trough? Why?

Name a few things you can do with a rock.

How would you feel if you had to spend the night in a stable with animals, like Mary, Joseph, and baby Jesus?

14

Dove

It is so nice and comfy up here.

The top rafters are always the warmest part of this barn, but tonight they're especially toasty. I think it's because some humans are down on the floor with oil lamps.

I'm not complaining! It's chilly outside. My feet were freezing, and the extra warmth is keeping my eggs safe in the nest under me. Thank the Lord God—tonight we will be snug!

An hour ago it was loud and chaotic in here. That young woman was making a bit of noise. The young man kept running around trying to help and make her nest comfortable. Poor man. The mother cows and donkeys in the stalls know more about birthing little ones than he does. Why don't humans just hatch their young out of eggs like I do? It would be a lot easier. Not to mention quieter. The other animals got nervous with all the unfamiliar noise and activity. I thought that donkey would never quiet down with all his braying. And the cows kept stamping and bellowing.

Just when I thought it couldn't get any worse, the baby started crying! But He was so cute. His little cries sounded all shivery. His mother wrapped Him up quickly and held Him close. I couldn't bear to hear that little one sounding so upset. My motherly instincts kicked in, and I started to coo. That's how I quiet *my* little ones. I don't know if it was because He heard my lovely coos or was being held by His dear momma, but that tiny thing quieted and went right to sleep. Shhhh. *Coo.*

They've been sleeping for a while now. As the peace and warmth of the barn settled in, we all relaxed after the excitement.

Looking down at the beautiful young momma with her precious new baby, I feel glad to be a mother like her. What a miracle!

How special to see that baby being born! But I wonder, Why have the baby here, surrounded by animals with a simple dove like me overhead? Where are the other people?

Well, one thing's for sure: whatever else happens in this baby's life, I'm glad He has a loving momma and papa.

What do you think the stable smelled and sounded like?

How would you have comforted baby Jesus that night?

How do you think Mary felt about giving birth around animals?

15
Blanket

It's been a long journey from Nazareth to Bethlehem. Everyone's tired. But that's when I do my best work! I may be just a humble blanket, but God has given me a purpose. I've protected the backs of donkeys, been laid on the ground as a bed for travelers, and been thrown around the shoulders of people in need of protection against the wind and rain. I may not have a real name, like Mary or Joseph, but some people have called me Cozy. Yet not since I was first woven have I ever had a day like today!

For the last few days, I've worked hard to soften the long donkey ride for a mother-to-be named Mary. I was pleased that I brought comfort to her tired back when she sat on me during the day and wrapped herself up in me at night. Today I've been given the honor of holding her newborn baby in my folds! But this little boy is not just any baby. His name is Jesus and He's the Son of God! There aren't words big enough and beautiful enough to really describe what it's like to be this close to God Himself.

As a blanket, one of my special qualities is to take the shape of whatever I cover. I wonder, Is that what it must be like to be a baby who is human and God at the same time? I mean, today God, who is bigger than the sky, is covering the world with His love in a special way. He's taking the shape of a baby. If I had a mouth, it would be open in wonder!

I'm so thankful God uses not only people but also animals and even *things* to comfort and share His love with the world. I may be old and starting to tatter, but out of all the blankets God could have chosen, He chose me to keep Jesus warm in this drafty stable, to help soothe Him when He cries and cuddle Him close in the special kind of hug only blankets can give. I may be just a little piece of fabric, woven from the wool of a lamb, but today I get to cradle Jesus, a baby that people will one day call Savior. What a wonderful gift God has given me—and the entire world!

If you have a favorite blanket—and it could talk—what memories would it tell you about?

Since Jesus experienced growing up as a child just like you, what might you ask or tell Him?

How has God comforted you?

16
Angel in the Sky

He's arrived! He's here! God's Son has come to earth! There's nothing in all God's creation that could keep me—and every other angel in heaven—from singing out the good news! What an amazing God we serve. He loves people so much that He has sent His own Son to live on earth with them. Songs of thanks and praise, wonder and awe, just keep tumbling from my lips. And God's glory, the light that shines around me, may be glowing even brighter than usual!

I know my excitement may be a bit overwhelming for the human beings below me. After all, most of them have never seen an angel, let alone an entire host of us, singing at the top of our lungs! But we just couldn't help ourselves. A song like this is so full of joy that all of heaven couldn't contain it. It simply had to spill out of heaven down onto the earth!

I tried to calm the shepherds watching their sheep in the fields below us and let them know why the heavens appeared to be bursting with glee. I shouted from the skies, "Do not be afraid. I bring you good news. It will bring great joy for all the people. Today in the town of David a Savior has been born to you. He is the Messiah, the Lord" (Luke 2:10–11 NIRV).

I wanted the shepherds to understand what was going on. But I also wanted them to go and see God's gift for themselves. When they do, I'm sure their hearts will be singing songs of praise, just like we are. Honestly, I think there'll be songs about God's Son echoing around the world from this day on throughout eternity.

One day soon, the baby who's just been born, Jesus, will be old enough to speak for Himself—and for His Father. I've been God's messenger since the moment of my creation. But when I deliver a message, people see an angel, not God Himself. Now that will change! When this child grows up and people see Him and hear Him speak, they'll see God, hear God's own words, and see God's love in action. As I said, how could I possibly keep my heart from singing on a day like this?

Why do you think we sing songs at Christmas?

If you could sing a song to Jesus on the day He was born, which would it be?

What would be your favorite part of an angel's job?

17
Lamb

"SeBAAstian! SeBAAAAstian …" My mother's voice woke me up. When I opened my eyes and heard all the singing, I couldn't believe I'd almost slept through it. Of course, I'm still young, so I pretty much sleep through anything. But there was music coming from the skies and bright lights overhead. The lights looked like giant fireflies or dancing stars or—don't laugh at me for saying this—people with wings! Whatever they were, I'd never seen anything like it. For a moment, I thought I was still dreaming.

But then I heard my shepherd's voice. "Everyone up!" he said. "Let's go!"

So that's exactly what we did—the entire flock. It didn't matter that it was the middle of the night. When our shepherd speaks to us, we listen. And we do what he says. We know we can trust him because he takes such good care of us. He leads us to food and fresh water so we always have enough to eat. He protects us from wild animals that might hurt us. And he always knows the way home.

Me? Not so much. My sense of direction doesn't work very well. I'm always getting turned around, so I just follow whoever is in front of me. If I were on my own, I'd probably wander in circles all day. Or I'd get distracted by a butterfly and when I looked up, the whole flock would have moved on. Yup, I'd be lost without my shepherd. Literally.

But my shepherd doesn't just lead me; he loves me. I know because he ruffles the wool on my neck when he sees me and he always calls me by my name. He's the one who first named me SeBAAstian. He named my mom BAAbs. He's fun like that. He loves me and I love him right back.

So off we go, as quick as we all can, across the rocky hills to a town called BAAthlehem. Or something like that. Even though it's dark and I don't know the way, I'm not afraid. As long as I stick close to my shepherd, I know I'll end up exactly where I'm supposed to be.

Have you ever petted a lamb? What did it feel like? If not, what do you think it might feel like?

What are some ways that shepherds help keep sheep, like SeBAAstian, safe and healthy?

Jesus called Himself the Good Shepherd. From what you know about shepherds, why do you think He took on this nickname?

18
Shepherd Boy

Come and see! Come and see! That's what the angel told us to do! He said—

Sorry, I guess I'm getting ahead of myself. A little while ago I was sitting on a hill outside Bethlehem with the other shepherds. The moon was out, the wind was a little chilly, and I was helping watch the sheep out in the fields. I've been a shepherd for as long as I can remember, so I'm pretty good at it by now.

Anyway, there we all were, trying to stay warm, when suddenly a big, bright light shone in the sky! To be honest, I was a little scared. I'd never seen anything like it. Out of the light came a heavenly voice, and it was speaking to *us*! Once our eyes adjusted, we saw that the voice belonged to an angel. He told us not to be afraid, that he brought great news: in the town of Bethlehem, a Savior had *just* been born, and His name was Jesus! The angel told us we would find the baby wrapped in cloth and lying in a manger—a *manger*? That seems weird for a Savior, doesn't it? None of us could speak, but we knew we had to go and see this Savior the angel told us about, so we all ran toward Bethlehem.

This is incredible! What am I going to say when I meet the Savior of the world? I guess He *is* a baby, so He probably wouldn't understand me anyway. Oh, this is so exciting!

Wait a second. Should I really go in there? I mean, if this is the Savior—the One who will rescue God's people—is what I'm wearing okay? All I have are these rough and dirty shepherd's clothes. It doesn't seem right to meet the Savior dressed like *this*. I'm getting nervous but still excited!

But then, that's what the angel told us to do. Wow, that was amazing … He said to go and find the baby in the manger, so that's what we're doing. This must be part of God's plan. I don't know why He chose *us*, but I'm so thankful He did.

I'm going to do it. I'm going to go meet the Savior …

What do you think life was like for the shepherds living outside Bethlehem? Would you want to try it?

How would you feel if an angel lit up the entire sky just to talk to you?

If you'd met baby Jesus that night, what would you have seen or said?

19

Simeon

Today God's promise to me has come true!

Many years ago the Lord spoke to me through His Holy Spirit. He told me I would not die until I had seen the Messiah—the Savior of the world—with my own eyes! Every day I have waited to meet the Messiah. For years I have waited … and waited …

I have lived in Jerusalem for many, many years. I remember a time before the Romans came, when Israel was a peaceful place. I remember when the Romans invaded our land and took over God's people. I remember how some people even began to doubt God's faithfulness … but I never lost hope that God would send His Son to rescue our people.

As time went by, I wondered about the moment when I would finally meet God's Son. Many powerful men have visited Jerusalem over the years, but none have been the promised Messiah. And so, I have waited … and waited …

Then *today* I heard God's voice telling me to go to the temple. I knew the voice was the very Spirit of God speaking, so I hurried off. I wasn't sure what I was going to find, but I knew God wanted me there for a reason.

As I was walking slowly through the temple courtyards and praying, I saw a young couple with their newborn Son. They were bringing the child to be blessed by the priests, just as God's Law commands. When I saw their baby boy, I was suddenly filled with joy, for I knew at once that *He* was the Messiah! I can't explain how the Holy Spirit showed me—I just knew!

I hurried to the couple as fast as my old legs would take me. I startled them. Imagine me, an old man with tears streaming down my face, fairly rushing up and asking if I could hold their Son! They said they had named Him Jesus.

I praised God for fulfilling His promise to me, and I declared loudly the great things this child would one day accomplish. I blessed the parents, then told the young mother that their Son would also face great challenges and suffering but that all of it would be to fulfill God's plan—not just for Israel but for the entire world!

For the rest of my days, I will praise God for giving me the chance to meet His Son!

How do you handle waiting for things?

Why do you think Simeon was an old man before he finally met Jesus?

If you were Mary and Joseph, how would you feel about the things Simeon said Jesus would do?

20
Anna

I know this temple better than I know my own heart. For more than fifty years, ever since my husband died, I've sheltered myself within these holy walls. Early every morning until late into the night, I've fasted and prayed right here. I've begged for understanding, wept over the loss of the man I loved, and praised God for the promises He has kept—for how He's provided for me, a poor widow, for so many years.

Like all God's people of Israel, I've prayed for the day God promised would come, the day a Savior would arrive to deliver us from our sins. Today is that day! The Messiah is here!

I overheard Simeon speaking to a young couple who had brought their little baby to the temple to present Him to the Lord. Simeon was thanking God for the baby that the mother held in her arms. I took one look at the child, and I too knew Simeon's words were true. God told me so!

Although I'm an old woman, God still chooses to use me as a prophetess. That means He sometimes whispers a message that I need to pass on to others. I shared my message—words of hope and joy—with the couple and the people around me. I think the Savior's mother felt a sense of peace in hearing from Simeon and me.

All these years, I've remained in this temple to stay close to God. But I never imagined being this close—close enough to see Him, to touch Him, and to sing over Him. My wrinkled arms may be weak and my legs unsteady with age, but right now I feel like I could run and skip and dance as wildly and freely as a child! Perhaps God has kept me alive for eighty-four years just so I could see the wonder of this very special day.

When I was still a young woman, God called me to this temple. Now, as an old woman, He's calling me outside, into the streets of Jerusalem. I have to tell everyone I meet the wonderful news! Our Savior has finally come—and His name is Jesus!

Who is your favorite older person? Why?

If God can use an old woman to tell other people about Jesus, do you think He can use someone your age? How?

If someone asked you about Jesus, what would you say?

21

Young Astronomer

I'm going to Israel! Me, an apprentice to the magi, who is still just learning!

I still can't believe it. Last night I was on the roof of the magi's tower, gazing at the stars like we usually do, and I saw the most bizarre thing in the sky. It looked sort of like a blazing planet. It was the second time I'd seen it, but no one else saw it last time. I'm pretty sure it's a sign!

I went running to fetch my teacher to come see it. But who do you think should be visiting the magi's tower but our new king? With the queen mother!

I thought I would be in trouble for running and yelling, but the king wanted to see the sign too, so we all went to the roof. Our ruler agreed it might be a sign from the gods to celebrate his becoming king. But my teacher explained that it had to be for the King of the Jews in Israel. Some old prophets—Daniel and Balaam—had predicted that one day a very special King would be born to Israel, and when He was born, a new star would rise.

At first our king was disappointed the sign wasn't for him, but then he became excited too. He wanted to gather some camels right then and go greet this new King. If Israel's God could make new stars appear, then he wanted to be friends with that whole country. Maybe their God would look with kindness on his kingdom.

But the queen mother said it was too dangerous for our king to make that kind of journey without a large group for protection—and that showing up with soldiers might accidentally start a war. He agreed, and then I could see an idea forming in his mind. He looked right at me with a big smile on his face.

So now *I'm* part of this group of wise men heading west to Israel to take royal gifts to this new King—bags of gold and rare spices and the most expensive perfumes. My teacher is coming too, along with many others. We'll be gone for months—who knows how long? I'm so excited!

Who could this King be?

Why do you think everyone was so excited by the strange light in the sky? Would you have been excited or scared?

If the king had asked you to take the journey, would you have wanted to go? Why?

What miracles do you think God is showing us today?

22
The Star

See that group traveling down there? They're magi and they're keeping a close eye on me, following my lead. It's not hard to do because I'm *pretty* hard to miss. This is all part of God's plan and why He created me to suddenly appear in the night sky.

Let me back up for a minute …

I'm part of a prophecy, or a series of predictions, dating back hundreds of years. God has been planning to send His Son, Jesus, to earth as a Savior for all people. He loves the world so much! One of the ways people will know the time has come, and how to find His Son, is to watch where I point.

When God was ready, He made me to suddenly shine so brilliantly in the sky—like a flash of a comet or a blazing planet—that people such as the curious magi down there couldn't *help* but notice me.

"A new star!" they proclaimed. Now they're eagerly heading west into the unknown on a journey to find a newborn King. They're right; they just have no idea how important this young King will be to them—to everyone!

What do you do when you meet a king? A King who is so favored that a new star like me appears in the sky to announce His birth? No one is quite certain, because this has never happened before. But these men are wise. They're planning to go worship. And they're respectful, so they've brought treasure to give as gifts when they find Him … *if they find Him.*

So off we go! I'm slowly gliding along in the sky, shining my heavenly light in this very special purpose for God. I shine so brightly, they can even see me during the day! How fun to watch the travelers and towns below. What a fantastic adventure we're all taking!

I feel a certain responsibility for these dedicated men. I want to be sure they don't lose their way or grow weary. I am full of love for them for leaving all they know, setting out in faith to follow these sparks from God: me in the sky and the one in their hearts.

Why do you think God used a star to announce the birth of Jesus?

How many other people might have seen the star and missed it?

What other things made by God show His power and love for us?

23
Camel

I sure have been walking for a long time, but I don't mind. My long legs are good for this sort of thing.

Before this journey began, I was living in the stables of a king in a land far, far away. I loved having people visit me, and I especially enjoyed carrying the king around his kingdom. Then one day the king told me I was going on a long journey to a distant land. I would carry an old teacher who was entrusted to take a whole bunch of treasure to a new King in Israel. I had no idea how far away Israel was … but I was about to find out!

Once we left the palace, we followed a striking bright light in the sky as we traveled across the dry and sometimes lonely desert. Luckily, my big, broad feet are good for walking across gravel and sand. All the while, I was bearing the old teacher on my back and leading the other camels on the way to visit this new King. Being a camel, I didn't need much food or water; the large humps on my back store all the energy I need for a long journey. As we traveled through deep valleys and tall mountains and I took in the amazing sights, I kept blinking my long eyelashes to keep the sand out of my eyes.

Eventually we came to a huge, wonderful city. There, the kind teacher patted my head and assured me that our journey was nearly over. He and his student went into a grand palace to speak with a king. I was sure this was *the* King, but when they came out, the teacher said we had a little farther to go. I didn't mind.

We saddled back up and set off for the little town. The star led us toward a small town just down the road from the big city.

After walking for months and months, my feet are starting to tire, and my humps need nourishment. While the teacher and his student have been very kind to me and the other camels, I could use some rest. We're almost at the little town now. I sure hope the teacher and his student can finally meet this new King! I wonder who He is!

Would you want to have a camel as a pet? Why or why not?

When you're traveling, what do you miss from home?

Why do you think many people still didn't know about baby Jesus being born?

24
Wise Man

It's time for me to return home from the greatest journey of my life! I am weary but also amazed at what I have seen. May I tell you about it?

It all began months and months ago, when my young student showed me a bright new star in the night sky. I determined that this star signaled the fulfillment of a prophecy that the God of the Israelites would one day send a special King of the Jews. My own king was curious. He decided to send me, along with other wise men (my student included), to search for this new King and take Him great gifts of gold, incense, and oil to honor His arrival. So we loaded up a caravan with valuable treasures and set off for the faraway land of Israel.

The journey was long and tough—much harder than I expected. I made sure to keep a sword close by in case we were attacked by bandits. Every night we camped under the night sky and gazed in awe at the bright star that continued to guide us on our path.

After months of traveling, the star finally led us to the large city of Jerusalem. We were brought before King Herod in his spectacular palace. (I must admit, it was even grander than the palace of our own king!) Herod asked us why we magi had come to Israel. I told him we were following a star to meet the new King of the Jews. When Herod heard this, he seemed interested—but also a little concerned. Herod's advisers said this new King was probably in the nearby town of Bethlehem. He instructed me to bring word back when we found Him.

In Bethlehem, we actually found this King of the Jews. I couldn't believe it—He was just a boy! Nonetheless, we were overcome with thankfulness at reaching Him after such a long journey. I wasn't expecting to feel this way, but we wanted to bow down before Him. We gave the boy's mother and father the treasures we'd brought. They seemed astonished at it all—our arrival and our gifts for the young King.

The night before we left, God spoke to me in a dream, telling me not to trust Herod and to return to my kingdom by a different route.

So that is what we are doing. Who knows how long it will take us to return home? However long, it will be worth it to protect this young King.

What would you like about following a star?

How do you think Mary and Joseph felt when the group arrived with all the gifts for their young Son, Jesus?

If you were going to give Jesus a gift, what would it be and why?

25
Donkey

Clip-clop, clip-clop, clip-clop … I like to imagine that every step I take plays a little tune. It helps the miles pass more quickly on this long journey. I can't wait until I *clip-clop* around that final bend and see home up ahead! I've missed sleeping under my favorite sycamore tree. I remember when a ripe piece of fruit would plop to the ground, sometimes waking me from a deep sleep. Mmm … I can almost taste the seedy sweetness of a freshly fallen fig from my favorite tree. It'll be so good to be home!

Not that I'm complaining. I've been on the adventure of a lifetime! Ever since I was a colt, I've helped Joseph carry branches and supplies back to his workshop. I may not be as big as a camel, but I'm really strong!

For years Joseph and I traveled no farther than the hills around Nazareth, working as a team. Then his wife, Mary, joined our family. Soon she was riding on my back as we *clip-clopped* our way to Bethlehem. It was so nice to carry a person instead of a pile of wood. Mary would stroke the hair on my neck and hum a sweet little song, even when the road was rough and rocky.

Once we made it to Bethlehem, Jesus was born. That brought our family to a total of four—including me, of course. Then we traveled together to Jerusalem, and then on to the distant country of Egypt. By the time we get home, our little family will have traveled around a thousand miles! That's more *clip-clops* than I could ever count.

We may be headed home, but our adventure isn't over. After all, there's a new child in the house! Who knows who Jesus will grow up to be? I wonder if He'll like to ride on my back. Will He share figs with me? Will He grow up to be a carpenter, like Joseph? Whatever adventure lies ahead for little Jesus, whether He stays close to home or journeys far away, I hope He'll travel the road ahead the same way I have—one step at a time, with a song in my heart, and in the company of the people I love.

What's the farthest you've ever traveled from home? How would your trip have been different if you'd had to ride a donkey?

What part of the Christmas story is your favorite? Why?

How does God sending Jesus make a difference in your life today?

Why Did God Send Jesus as a Baby?

God created everything—from the stars to the bugs—and it was good. The first two people, Adam and Eve, lived in a beautiful garden. They knew God very well and were close to Him.

But … Satan is a destroyer, so he lied to Adam and Eve. They didn't obey God, and their sin of disobedience broke the relationship they enjoyed with God. They could no longer be as close because He is holy.

This made God very sad. He made a plan to one day bring them back into relationship with Him because He loved them so much! He would send a Redeemer to save them by showing them how to restore their relationship.

Through the years and years and years, God showed who He was in the promises He made—and kept—in the lives of His people:

Noah …

Abraham …

Ruth …

Daniel …

Rahab …

and King David.

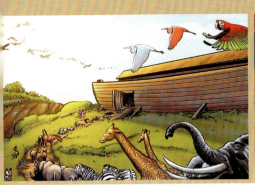

After so many years, it was time to send this Redeemer who would save people from their sins. He wanted people to decide to stop sinning and follow Him.

God sent His Son, Jesus, to earth both to be God and to live as a human. God wanted people to understand who He is through the words and actions of His Son.

Jesus was born as a baby to two regular people, Mary and Joseph, in a not-so-regular way. He came as a helpless baby and not a full-grown person. By letting people care for Him, He showed how humble He was. He also learned about all the things we go through. His miraculous birth was the first of many ways God showed His great love for us, the people He created.

When Jesus grew up, He showed God's love for us in the way He treated people, the lessons He taught, and the miracles He performed. Jesus cared for everyone He met and shared His message of how much God loves us.

Jesus invited people to trust in Him, then follow Him in the way they live their lives. He would save people from their sins and restore their relationship with God. But not everyone believed Jesus was God's Son, and some hated Him.

Then … Jesus allowed Himself to be sacrificed on a cross for our sins. He died so we can be close to God again. Someone had to pay the price for our sins, and Jesus was willing. That was God's plan all along. That's why Jesus died on the cross.

Jesus' friends and followers were very sad, but He didn't stay dead! On the third day, He came back to life. He is alive today and is living in heaven. By His Spirit, He lives within people who trust in Him.

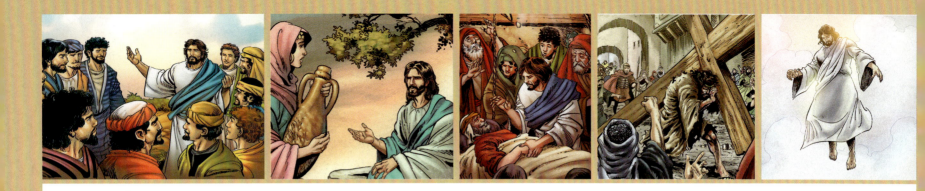

We can know we will live forever in heaven with Jesus when our life on earth is done, if we accept Him as our Savior and Redeemer.

That's why God sent Jesus as a baby—for you and me.

That's why Jesus died on the cross—for you and me.

Note to Adults

We hope you've enjoyed experiencing the story of Jesus' arrival through these twenty-five perspectives. Children already feel awe and wonder on a deep level. When we consider this familiar story—at least, familiar to us as adults—through their eyes and the viewpoints of the other witnesses to the miracle, our own sense of curiosity and the miraculous is restored.

If you would like to continue exploring these stories, there are numerous *The Action Bible* resources geared to the ages of your children:

The Action Storybook Bible: ages 4–8
The Action Bible Easter: ages 5 and up
The Action Bible: Heroes and Villains: ages 8 and up
The Action Bible Anytime Devotions: ages 8 and up
The Action Bible Study Bible ESV: ages 8 and up

For even more *The Action Bible* resources, go to TheActionBible.com.
Additionally, the entire Christmas story can be found in the Bible in Matthew 1–2 and Luke 1–2.

THE MOST EPIC STORY EVER TOLD!

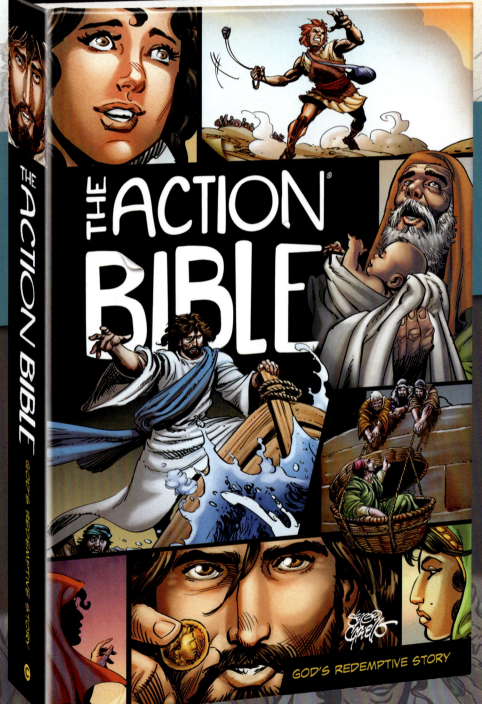

Every page in **THE ACTION BIBLE EXPANDED EDITION** sparks excitement to explore God's Word. Beginning with stories from the Old Testament through to fascinating details about the life of Jesus, readers of all ages become witnesses to God's incredible redemptive story.

- **FEATURING 128 NEW PAGES** of illustrations for additional & expanded Bible storylines.

- **ENHANCED STORYLINES** that come together in the most complete illustrated Bible ever captured in one book.

- **EVERY PAGE SPARKS EXCITEMENT** to explore God's Word & know Him personally.

HERO or VILLAIN?
YOU DECIDE!

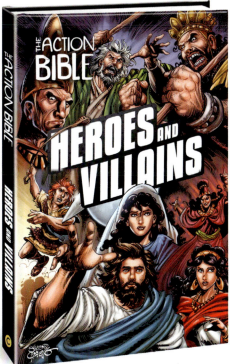

This all-new addition to **THE BESTSELLING ACTION BIBLE** line bursts with fun facts, surprising stories, and full-color art for every young reader who wants to become an expert on the greatest heroes and villains of God's Redemptive Story.

Available from David C Cook
and everywhere books are sold

DAVID **C** COOK